Wings of Poesy

Poetry Anthology of INNSÆI International
Lit Fest

Chief Editors

Dr Tejaswini Patil Dange
Mr Orbindu Ganga

Executive Editors

Dr Kalpana Gangatirkar
Ms. Aditi Barve
Dr Sushmindarjeet Kaur

Editor and Compiler

Ms. Sweta Kumari

All Rights Reserved

Book: Wings of Poesy: Poetry Anthology of INNSÆI International Lit Fest, Goa, 2022
Published: Notion Press
Copyright © May 2023
Book Formatting: Sweta Kumari
Cover Design: Sweta Kumari

DISCLAIMER

We have tried our best to check for plagiarism in the write-ups of all the contributing co-authors to this book. However, if something has escaped from our eyes and if plagiarism is found later on, we shall not be liable for the same. As we have asked all the co-authors to submit their original and unpublished works. Our bond and relationship are based on utmost good faith with them.

Dr Tejaswini Patil Dange
Chief Editor

Dr Kalpana Gangatirkar
Executive Editor

FOREWORD

We need peace, unity, empathy and a shared vision of a harmonious world for a brighter future of humanity. The world is surrounded by chaos and fear. Life is characterized by speed and competition, power, want and lust. Even though we achieve everything still we face anxiety and negativity. It is the need of time to promote peace and stop violence, to show more love and empathy to our planet. We should sing songs of peace and happiness. This anthology is an attempt to search and pervade peace in all spheres of life. It was really a pleasing experience to compile and edit the beautiful poems evoking peace. The present anthology exhibits varied and rich emotions of mature poets.

Abhinav discusses various boundaries and the fences in which people live. His poem expresses a melancholy mood with the expression "nothing changes". He thinks that we are acting as if we are united but at heart, we are full of fear. At the end, the poet becomes optimistic and states "unity is required to establish serenity". He defines harmony as "no-harm-any".

Kamei's poem "September 2020" is an excellent example to show the chaos created out of extreme violence. It makes the readers restless. Can violence be any time justified? The poem is a manifestation of order lessness in life and so in word order. The poem is like a brilliant puzzle piece, yet is has safeguarded its poetic sense.

Prof. Basudev Paul's "humanity Cries in War" is a criticism of war for power. Power is corrupt, power makes, no matter which kind of societal structure we live-in. He asks question if poetry is born out of war what about peace? "The Swing" is an extremely beautiful poem that oscillates between fear of war and bliss of life. It starts with an empty swing and ends with a child running happily towards the swing. It answers the human kind needs peace and pleasure by exampling the child running to swing even in fearsome war surroundings.

"A Little Pause" by Debdoot Mukherjee views death as just a pause rather than an end. As every black cloud has a silver lining every ending has a new and fresh start. Humans search rays of hope and happiness even in the darker interiors. Indran's "Eternal Bonding" speaks about human relations. She seems to view such bonding in high regards. For human beings real identity is rooted in humanity.

Jasnoor's "Free Dandelions" visualizes the tiny flowers spreading unlimited bliss. It underlines "Nature is peace". Kalpana Gangatirkar's poem Pursuit of Peace is an attempt to find out serenity and peace. The peace in real sense cannot be found in fame, and name or human relations or even spiritual pursuits. Peace is making agitating souls happy .

Laxman Rao defines poetry as the innate voice, thoughts shaped in purity wise words and witty verse. "Woman thy name is surviving and rebuilding", --- Isn't it truly 'The Tough Granny' by Mandakini Bhattacharya comments? The poem takes about the powerful ability of women to fight and survive through violence. Meenakshi Goswami's "Sanguinity" explains that the nature's world is beautiful and the human world is broken and full of violence but still we have to walk forward with cheerfulness.

"Torn Vest Owner" by Nitusmita Saikia is an astonishing criticism of romanticism of poverty. She bashes the views on poverty through rose tinted glass and vividly presents rather harsh reality. She appeals the poets and readers "will you come to see us in our little sky, to hear the untold story of our torn vest owner"?

Dr. Patil in her poem "Delightful Destination" celebrates the power of silence and pauses in nature. She believes that they connect us to the ocean, trees, and future, offering a serene destination in the lap of Nature. Whereas Dr. Patil's another poem, "The Bullet" exposes violence against women, their resilience, and the suppression of their voice questioning if a bullet can truly extinguish their spirit.

'The Eleventh Hour' by Orbindu Ganga states that arts survive through horrified violence. This poem is memorable for the use of words. Pankhuri Sinha in her ironical and sarcastic tone comments the present-day situation in her 'Peace is Hostage to Love".

"Buddha, We Need You Again" by Ms. Barve is a plea for the teachings of Buddha to be revived. It urges us to understand cause and effect, seek inner peace, and cultivate compassion towards all beings. And another poem of Ms. Barve titled "Life starts at Forty" captures the author's experience of feeling unaccomplished and disliking themselves due to over thinking. It celebrates women as the light of the rising sun, deserving of peace, joy, and a life lived on their own terms.

In "Mellifluous Musings: A Healing to Scars", Ms. Sweta, touches upon the resilience and empowerment of women in the face of adversity celebrating the indomitable spirit of women who rise above subjugation and oppression. The poem conveys the importance of individual voices coming together in harmony to validate and uplift women, creating a world of self-esteem and freedom.

The poem "The Voice of an unloved lover" expresses the grief of the lover and his search for inner peace which might recover harmony "Each Visit" by Parneet Jaggi is a visual expression of nostalgia. Dr. Saroj Kanta Dash's "To an African Poet Friend" is about unjust treatment and discrimination based on caste, class, race and colour all over the world. It is a gentle and friendly consolation of one friend to other saying "Hearts are not coloured" "Humanity and Peace" by Shalini Yadav asks us to be ambassador of peace and harmony.

The poet Shikdar Mohammed Kibriah wishes to linger in his dreams of love, peace and beauty. Dr. Sharbani Chakravorty's shades of life capture beauty of nature. Shweta Sing's 'Your Two Selves' reflects inner conflict of what man does and what he really wants. The same idea of 'conflict' is developed further by Dr. Sigma in her poem.

Dr. Sumangla Pateriya's 'Prayer for Peace' is an earnest prayer to Almighty Dr. Kaur believes that Peace should not remain only a word, but should be 'a state of mind', our 'act of performance' and 'a state of bliss'. Dr. Sunanda Shelake states that women through their poetry could create storms of words. Lt. Vinodkumar wonderfully discusses the beauty and the superiority of human heart.

I am glad to handover such a memorable collection of different perspectives penned by acclaimed poets and hope you find peace and bliss through it.

Dr Tejaswini Patil Dange   **Dr Kalpana Gangatirkar**
   Chief Editor   **Executive Editor**

Table of Contents

Abhinav Brar

Abhinav Brar is a Commerce Student at University of Windsor. He is really passionate aboutwriting and photography. The anthologies *His and Her Summer* and *That Sapphire Night* contain some of his earlier writing, mainly poetry. He also has a short story selected to be published in "Tales of our times".

Harm Any (Harmony) Over War

Challenging to stick together,
Humbling to be left alone.
Acting that we stand united forever.
Under the influence,
degrading the people over the fence,
Humanity losing against religion.
Acting like we are not all the same and not acting on ending
this tradition.
Resting on others to amend, or resting like we don't need to
change.
Yesterday was the same as today, the time didn't change.

Despite we act in spite, being alone is what we fright.
Emptying the ego,
vague familiarities become clear.
Embracing the dissimilarities, we fight this rite.
not keeping grudges but letting go,
distance will be overcome, so will be the fear.
Easier to find harmony,
remembering not to harm any.

Saffron stand for sacrifice, so should you,
in order to cure this idiopathic disease of hatred.
Not allowing people to live how they wanted.
Grain on the fingers from these wars, we need to cease fire.
Heading towards serenity, unity is required.
~ **Abhinav Brar**

Achingliu Kamei

A short story writer, poet, children's writer, creative writing mentor, and ultra-runner, Achingliu Kamei teaches Literature at DU. Her latest publication is *Songs of Raengdailu*, a book of poems (2021). Several of her poems are published in anthologies and journals in the USA, Canada, Singapore, and India.

SEPTEMBER 2020

Justice for cry we
2020 of September on gain incident another
web the of spinning clever the in lost
others the like kind her–fate same generations
fields in found well water near
garden backyard theirin found was she
off cut hands, legs crushed, face her on thrown acid
off cut tongues her naked her paraded
'thugs,' nameless the, securely hidden, known not names their
intent evil with come had they day that - premeditated -
terrified too
were cries her heard who ones the
sons two daughters three had she
fields their on ripening corns love to used they
traumatized children her- fields corn on
shines sun the of light the
again same the be never will music the
day that music Hindustani to listening were
they when home brought was mother their of body bloodied
grave no - corns ripening seeing on
them reminds community their of helplessness
sari the of pallu the on run colours the when crack
face his will.

~ **Achingliu Kamei**

Basudev Paul

Captain Prof Basudev Paul has been teaching at Parimal Mitra Smriti Mahavidyalaya, Malbazar, Jalpaiguri, West Bengal, India. He has been commanding the English Department as a HoD since 1986, under North Bengal University (NBU). Dressed in poetical robes, Basudev searches thoroughly and wildly the ikigai of poetry. Among the rocks Paul finds the flint of spark that diffuses on the premises of creation. His poems speak with the imagination of the twenty first century. The diction, vivid imagery, and variegated moods glowingly communicate the messages of an aching desolation, plaguing the world. An offshoot of Nature, Paul puts in his best to carry the clarion voice of hope.

Humanity Cries in War

'Up up socialism, down down capitalism'
My infantile fancy couldn't catch the crux
Communism spread this say the world over
My adulthood strove to get the hang of it.

Jockeying for power goads the Elder Brother
To spread and spearhead aggression
To extend the power of the imperialism
The USA was infrared as the power of the baton.

What does God plan in the firmament of Putin?
Having tasted the luxuriance of power in
Born to see diplomacy from childhood
Attacking Ukraine has been an example of it.

Wresting the power from the Ukrainian soil
And establish the sovereignty by means foul
The Ukrainian people fought tooth and nail!
Putin has been raging in a power cauldron.

Reminded of Owen the 'the pity of war', fie!
Shelling in the warfare does no good to us
Humanity sighs on the blasted heath, moldy!
'Power corrupts, absolute power corrupts
Absolutely'!

Poetry was born in the ashes of world war I, and II.
But peace?
Owen, Sassoon, Brook, Blunden, all rotted

Danny Cherian

A teacher by profession, who loves to weave patterns of life, which are symphonies of the immortal universe. He loves to explore intimate souls living in harmony with eternity.

The Swing

Silently still, there a swing stood.
In a park near a distant wood.
None to sway in joy came there,
Or to sit, as one of a loving pair.

As lively leaves dried and fell,
Blew the wind close to tell.
A story, of bondage in human.
Inside walls, weeping for men.

Behind, the darkness of doors closed.
Crawled some forms their history paused.
A smile, hidden beneath, a precious mask,
Was all, the answer to the why, we ask.

Like portraits, painfully unfinished
Looked everyone to other they wished.
As gloom poisoned despair and with fire fed,
To be nearer was fear and to touch was dread.

Some reminded; the way of nature it is.
Another spoke, it's the wrath; a disease.
Yet, through the window peered the eyes out,
A vision that never failed in collective doubt.

To the swing, ran the careful child.
Her arms stretched wondrously wide.
A soft creak and into the rusty wind flew,
The mask that kept life frozen without a clue.

~ Danny Cherian

Debdoot Mukherjee

Debdoot Mukherjee teaches English in the Department of English, Bhangar Mahavidyalaya, University of Calcutta. His poems are his pieces of thoughts on life. The present poem tries to understand life and death as two inseparable identities in the journey towards eternity.

A Little Pause!

Night dawns upon me
As morning does on night
The flowers have started blooming
In the search for light
The light that waits for them
In the boundless ocean of rebirth
Forming waves of hope and happiness
Amidst the depth of dark interiors
That call forth innate fears
Of existential concerns
Seemingly uplifted identity
Whispering in the ears of the deaf
Snatching the inner brightness from the blind
Crossing horizons of bars
Into the eternity of voyagers
In search of time,
And the flirting truth
Death is just a pause.

~ Debdoot Mukherjee

Indrani Chatterjee

Indrani Chatterjee, an author, a self motivated writer and poet, a perfective homemaker and mother to her only autistic child. Even from the barred layer of felicity, her emotions occasionally well up to inundate the white in blue. Nothing is ceremonial in her revelation and approach, purely self motivated. She only wishes her readers to glide along with the rhythmic undulations of her penmanship.

Eternal Bonding

Where contemplation smites beyond terrestrial horizons
And arbitrary halo enlightens the spirit.
The inner chants percolates soul to evoke meditative silence,
It is there the splurge of divine evolvement originates an
eternal bonding I believe.

Where soul reaches out for soul and declines to look for
identity beyond humanity,
A slight relinquishment to initiate felicity of life in solidarity.
Where shades of mankind pervade ubiquitously to harmonise,
It is there the consummate success of eternal bonding lies.

From the womb of dark emanates the visionary domain,
Commuting Phases to make their eminence certain.
Life has its rollercoaster ride to interpolate crisis and
opulence side by side,
Though discrete in nature, still they embrace each other,
An eternal bonding with vicissitudes is taken into stride.

When spirit of a smith is deluged with paragon of imageries,
He nestles in the realms of aestheticism to impart his creative
deliveries.
It's the eternal bonding with aphorism to bridge the gap
between thoughts and expressions,
Rendering an amaranthine bliss with its iridescent
manifestation.

Eternal bonding perches on the surface where selflessness
never dies,

Jasnoor

Jasnoor is a student of BBA at Christ University, Bangalore. She is passionate about food and fitness. Creativity drives her. Her poems have appeared in several anthologies. She is also a badminton player.

Free Dandelions

Blades of grass
sway with the breeze,
free dandelions
ride the winds
free of mind's clutter,
the weights of life,
the worries and tiny thorn pricks,
pickpocketing grains from sacks,
rubbing the delicate hue of crimson petals,
teaching me to glide through the saturated airs
and enjoy life.

~ Jasnoor

Laxman Rao

L. Rao known as Laxman Rao, has his MA Litt English from Bangalore, he has been pursing poetry for the last 2 decades, who is a classist by choice while a modernist by mind, who weaves poetry with equal ease. He has recited poems in many Bangalore poetry festivals and has published poems in "POETS INTERNATIONAL" magazine and other international Facebook forums. Published his poetic debut as "THE WORLD WITHIN" and translated his belated friend's Telugu collection of poems as "THE SECRET SCRIPTURES OF LIFE". He brought in a self-publishing house as: "VERSESMITH PUBLISHERS". He is an avid reader and an intense writer. And his ideology towards Poetry is POETRY by itself, wherein most of his poems move around the poet's mindset his attributes, his entire gamut as a person and his persona with his poetic nuances and subtleties, which he gives life to. He has versed poetry in almost all forms and patterns, which he is very well versed off. He has worked in films in the script writing, screen play, and the direction dept, He is a multilinguistic person who speaks in 5 languages English, Telugu, Tamil, Kannada, and Malayalam. He is a poet, a script writer, publisher, and an entrepreneur, to sum it up in short.

When I Do Speak Poetry

When I do speak of poetry and poetics,
The poet in me speaks; whilst it's not me!

It's his language of mum minds; innate voice,
Where his emotions yield to expressions…
It's his ease in its eloquence to please,
Which a reader might reveal as he reads…
It's his perspective in its prescience;
Where concepts conceived or carved with essence…
It's creative calibre for the craft,
Where thoughts shape up in profound purity…
It's his wit; woven in verse- his wisdom
In what wordings vested, as jewel chest.

Poetry is the mirage of one's mind
The magic of words-refined and defined!

~ Laxman Rao

Mandakini Bhattacherya

Mandakini Bhattacherya is an Associate Professor in English at Fakir Chand College (Affiliated to University of Calcutta) Diamond Harbour, West Bengal, India. She is Teachers' Council Secretary at Fakir Chand College and Joint Secretary, Proyas, Sarsuna, a Women's NGO.

The Tough Granny

Geriatrics or gender,
or simply an innate talent to hang on to dear life
like the turtle or climbing perch, -
Something it is
that makes us women unique.
Else, I would have surely thrashed to death
somewhere in the journey
from childhood to tired womanhood -
giving, ripening, fattening,
nurturing my offsprings and kin -

Till the day I was left alone,
weak, doddering, seventy-three,
whom even a one-armed robber
could overpower - bludgeon, clobber -
crush the orbital bones with a screwdriver,
only to escape with some lucre,
while the family was away
to celebrate the Goddess of Lucre.

The police wait to hear my story
from lips bloodied and sutured -
They are sure I will survive -
once again.

~ **Mandakini Bhattacherya**

Nitusmita Saikia

Nitusmita Saikia is a bilingual writer from Assam, India. With poetry, she writes short stories, plays, quotes and articles. She has been writing for magazine like FM, GloMag, Tuck magazine, Innsaei and Sandhan, etc. Her poems have been published in many national and international anthologies etc.

Torn Vest Owner

Me and my torn vest,
Do you see,
The scattered holes and the broken threads...!
Nothing but stars and galaxies,
They are,
Adorning the little sky I have in my eyes,
Often see dreams there to console mere,
To lose all hopes from the so-called donated life.

Poor question would be if I ask
who am I? '
Nothing but the stone that been used,
To build the highway
where your Ferrari and Mercedes rides.

Little ostensibly naked is my child,
An epithet for poverty ridden existence,
Overwhelming inspiration if I am not wrong,
You paint my scorched dehydrated lips
You write poetry on my burning heels,
And speech on hunger, you deliver,
On speechless torn vest owner,
Maintaining all social morale distance.

What about the end of our life..!
I write with my child's tears now,
Kind of spring fest of holi
blood spilled over our iron pillows
And our roti,
Who knows now where we are,

Will you come to see us in our little sky,
To hear the untold story of torn vest owner?
~ Nitusmita Saikia

Pankhuri Sinha

Bilingual poet and story writer from India, who has lived in North America for 14 years and has two books of poems published in English, two collections of stories published in Hindi, five collections of poetries published in Hindi, with many more lined up. Has won many prestigious, national-international awards, has been translated in over twenty five languages. She has been published in many journals, anthologies, home and abroad. And has won several prominent national and international awards for her writings, has done residencies in Hungary and Bulgaria, participated in Tranas Litfest in Sweden.

Peace is Hostage to Love

Peace is hostage to love
On the broken roads
Once built with foreign collaboration
Where the militia, the mafia, the naxals
The guerillas, and even the Taliban smuggling themselves
Inside borders, hide out, sneak in
Mingling sometimes at the local tea stalls
With people and the system before the ambush and the kill
. . . .
Peace is hostage to love . . . .

Peace is hostage to the good old cry of development
Discrimination, disparity, distance!
On that dirt trail leading to the mud homes
Not too far away from the village school
With thatched roof that leaks in the rain
And where teachers serve meals better than teach classes
And where students aim to learn enough to sign their names
Where local toddy freely flows before paddy ripens
And women walk to the forest and to the market
To light up that fire, which cooks, and warms and illuminates
The broken wires of the govt electric pole
Just a few steps away, peace is hostage to bribery
Corruption, in a country which competes to have
The richest denizens of this world!
Peace is hostage to love!
Peace is hostage to empathy, sympathy,
Even humanity, tattered, battered

Seen molested in the long lines migrating

Dr. Parneet Jaggi

Dr. Parneet Jaggi is Associate Professor of English at Dr. B.R. Ambedkar Government College, Sri Ganganagar, Rajasthan, poet, editor, critic and novelist. She has five collections of English poems, 3 research books, *The Indelible Indianness, Matthew Arnold and the Bhagavad Gita* and *Social and Economic Values in the Teachings of Sikh Gurus* and has co-edited five books. Her historical fiction *The Call of the Citadel* (jointly authored with Vikram Singh Deol) won the Golden Book of the Year for Historical Fiction 2022, Ukiyoto award for Best Plot 2022 and Aazad International Award for Historical Fiction 2021. Her name appears in the 'Directory of Writers' in America's magazine Poets and Writers. She was declared the 'Poet of the Year 2019' and 'Critic of the Year 2019' by Destiny poets, Yorkshire, UK and won the Wingword Poetry prize (India) 2020 for her Punjabi poem.

Each Visit

Whistle of the train hints
I have been here.
Rustling of the mango leaves
shoves memories of my previous childhood.
Rainbow walking silently over the dying clouds
reminds me of the games I played near the Yamuna.
The temple bells, the hymn tunes,
enter the blood stream in less time than I can measure.
I have been here several times.
This earth has been my home
-countless times.
It hasn't changed.
Only I grow smart on each visit.

~ Dr. Parneet Jaggi

Dr. Sarojkanta Dash

Sarojkanta Dash is bilingual in English and Odia. As a writer, his areas of interest involve literary criticism, short fiction and poetry. He has already published a short story collection in Odia entitled Anuragara Basna (Fragrance of Love). It was published in 2010, and was well-acclaimed for having stories that explore into the 'technologies of the self'. He appears frequently in mainstream magazines and the newspapers. With this book, he makes his debut entry into the canon of English criticism. In fact, he received his Ph.D. from Sambalpur University for this work (title slightly changed) in 2012. A lecturer by profession, he has been teaching English since 1990.

To an African Poet Friend

Tight-lipped
You cannot scream
And seclusion is lost
When you talk so much
To yourself.

Hearts are not coloured.
The sky over the Himalayas
Kilimanjaro
And Scafell Pike
The Ganges, the Niles, the Congo
And the Thames
Is the same.

And dear one !
Is heart not the sky cover
Of humanity?

So, smile like the Sun
At dawn
And take the Mediterranean
By the horns
Thump your surfboard
On the Suez
And roar into the Indian Ocean.

Won't you talk
To the seagulls?
Won't you sing
Of the days

How we grew on the ashes
Of time?

Both
Miles apart
But bound together
By the colour of wounds!

No need to scream
When friends are around
A soft whisper
Can raise the dead.

~ Dr. Sarojkanta Dash

Shikdar Mohammed Kibriah

Pen-name SHIKDAR MOHAMMED KIBRIAH, originally named SHIKDAR GULAM KIBRIA, born on 1st July, 1968, in Sylhet, Bangladesh, Masters in philosophy, globally published, awarded and translated world renowned poet, essayist, story writer, translator, ambassador and philosopher. He is a bilingual poet and writer writing in Bangla and English. He is the founder and president of Poetry and Literature World Vision. His published books are so far 17. As a global poet and literary personality he often participates in world poetry conferences, International poetry festivals and literary conclaves. He is an ambassador of world peace, love and humanity appointed by different literary, cultural and poetic forums active globally. His writings are often published in world famous print and electronic magazines, journals, newspapers, websites, blogs, anthologies, TV, Radio and Channels. His works have been translated in 40 languages.

A Half Lying Moon

If my sense of dream would be a sensitivity
I could have a mild moon in my hand
Like a half lying fair lady.

I have a white pigeon living in my mind
That holds dreams of love, peace and beauty
In her white feather.
Even if I could not realize how a sensitive dream
Could be a song of human light
When our sensible deer is often bloodied
By a dream killer human tiger!

Who could believe in having a dreamy fruit
From this bad dream tree!
And who can conceive a dreamy child
And break her barrenness!
I won't return to this perceptive world
And will be hung up in my dreamt sky
As a half lying moon.
With a awakening sleep I'll have a dream
Of just picking----

~**Shikdar Mohammed Kibriah**

Dr Shrabani Chakravorty

Dr Shrabani Chakravorty Head, Dept.of English is presently posted at Govt. Vivekanand PG College Manendragarh district Koriya, Chhattisgarh. She has done MA English from Ravishankar University Raipur and later awarded Ph.D. from Guru Ghasidas University Bilaspur. Her specialisation is in Indian writing in English. She is a Research supervisor since 2015 at Atal Bihari Vajpayee University, Bilaspur. She has a long teaching experience of 34 years. She has published 32 Research papers in the journals and books of National and International repute. Her area of interest is writing and recitation of poetry in English Hindi and Bangla, short story writing, original quotes and storytelling. She has been writing poetry in hindi regularly for hindibhasha. com. She is an active member of ELTAI, INTACH, CETA, Aurobindo Society for academic activities. Her interest in social activities has been for more than 14 years, as an active member of Rotary International's Innerwheel club, Bilaspur, Maa Sharda Kanya Vidyapeeth, Podki Amarkantak, a school for Baiga tribe girls, Bengali Mahila Sangathan, Central Bengali Association Bilaspur.

Shades of Life

The bonding of the earth and sky
Around the verdure forests on all sides
The placid sunset reflects its image on the stream
The day recedes and gently the night brims.

Who has spread the golden rays at twilight?
Who has painted the river with flourishing hue?
The glorious landscape deep dark in the middle
Receives the blessings from above and boon from beneath.

Beautiful is the work of nature
Splendid the hands of Almighty
In lending the distinct shades of life
Through the sky above,
The woods around,
And the river flowing down.

~ Dr Shrabani Chakravorty

Paramita Adhikari

Paramita Adhikari is currently working as a SACT (State-Aided College Teacher) at the Department of English in Serampore Girls' College under the University of Calcutta. She is a passionate learner. Poetry is her constant companion. She loves travelling, reading and cooking.

The Voice of an Unloved Lover

Like an adept artisan, a lover erects the Taj Mahal of his love;
Like a skilled sailor, a lover holds the love-boats even in strong tide in strong hand enough;
But, if that lover is once unloved, can be devastating easily;
The flood of unwanted love can destroy everything terribly.
At last, one day, that lover gets very irritated and turns the eyes blind,
Then, that lover kills all will-power and takes the oath of not becoming kind.
In disgust, that lover closes all the doors of returning,
The cry of all the oppressors of the world seem trifle to that lover in revolting.
The way the colorful dreams of that lover spoil by the world's attack,
That lover's instilled desires turn into Hitler's horrible outrage in shock!
Once, on dry sands, that lover blooms bunch of flowers;
Water fills the aridity of the desert and new life engenders.
But, that lover becomes unvalued today, plucks and damages the flowers of the garden;
Now, to this poisonous world, that lover seems to be a burden.
That lover can drink desperation, dejection and distress;
That lover can eat like a hungry tiger all the stigma by society in an instant confesses.
Take a look at the history of the universe!
From time to time, through the scratch of those lovers' pen, outstanding rare love-sagas have been written in verse.
Think, if the pen of an unloved lover roars again, against the hypocrisy of society;

Dr Shweta Singh

Dr Shweta Singh is presently working in the capacity of the Assistant Professor in Jyoti Nivas College Autonomous Bangalore. She has ten years of teaching experience. Her area of interest is Dalit Literature in translation, gender studies and literary autobiographies.

Your Two Selves

Your two 'selves' live in my existence
One that knit the dreams and cherish them
Another that break them into pieces
And leave it to rot in tears

In trials of balancing these two
I lose my own self
Now the conflict of leaving you
And living with you torments my soul

Often, I brace to see beyond you
The life of my own
But, do I own a life, which can be called my own
Only shattered pieces left astray

The eyes, once cherished many dreams
Of bright sunshine, of love
Denied now even to exist with
Little sympathy and leftover warmth

I heard pragmatic distance helps
 Rekindle the dead souls
And fills the void left between you and me
To coexist together

Will it be ever possible to get a path
Between these two 'I''s of yours?
Over the horizon I imagine you
Calling my name beyond these two selves.

~ Dr Shweta Singh

Dr Sigma

Dr Sigma, a widely published Indian poet, is currently the HoD of English at VTMNSS College inTrivandrum. She worked for Oman Ministry of Manpower as a Faculty of English. Sigma's poems appeared in many anthologies and received Mirabhai Literary Award from the Organization of United Working Journalist Forum, supported by Public Relations Department, Puri, and Govt of Odisha in 2016. Sigma is a recipient of Cochin Literary Fest Prize-2019. She published many poetry books and is often invited as a poet delegate to various prestigious national and international poetry festivals.

Conflicts

Conflicts among us
help to realize
the art of war
I hear a great deal of talks,
about peace.
I lock my mind.

Now whom should I listen,
I scribble verses of life
That may help you, to find
the lost you in the war field
I would still feel you
and I undress my pain, like whirlwind
and I wait for you
with infinite love
in this journey...

~ Dr Sigma

Dr. Sumangla Pateriya

Dr. Sumangla Pateriya, Associate Professor, English Govt. Hamidia College Bhopal. A number of research papers published in national and international journals. Few of her poems published in international peer reviewed journals. Major areas of interest in research are Indian ethos and Indian Writing in English.

A Prayer for Peace

The wrath of Ares, the fury of Mars
A spate of blood, millions of scars.
The torrid storm and ocean of tears,
Heart wrenching wails of an orphan's fears,
The petty pretense of pelf and power,
Brutal shattering of dreams and ivory towers,
The din and roar of desolate streets,
The horrid horror of horrendous fleets.
Ruthless ravage, vanquished Man,
Valiant soldiers, dying in vain.
Prayers for peace, no more savage slaughter plead,
O merciful Lord, let not the Mother's holy heart bleed.

~ Dr. Sumangla Pateriya

The storms
Striking every moment of CREATION!

~ Dr. Sunanda Shelake

Lieutenant Vinodkumar Ashok Pradhan

Lieutenant Vinodkumar Ashok Pradhan: Belongs to Kavalapur in Sangli district. He has taken education through many adversities. Presently he is working as Assistant Professor of English and NCC Officer (ANO) in Sadashivrao Mandlik Mahavidyalaya, Murgud in Kolhapur for last 17 years. Teaching, Photography and Composing poetry in English, Hindi and Marathi is close to heart.

My Heart

O my breath please go slow
My Heart is so tender to bear the flow

O you wind don't make noise
My Heart has its own special pace…

O you all fragrances just go to hell
My Heart has its own unique smell…

O you people you go to shrines so special?
My Heart goes anywhere makes the place its own chapel…

O famous wonders don't much boast
My Heart can beat you more wonderful toast…

O you autumn don't be proud your seasonal greenery
My Heart is always rich with its own finery…

Do you find all pleasures in nature?
My Heart gives me the same kind of stature…

O you all rhythms you keep beating best?
My Heart has the soothing notes while taking rest…

You say the universe is so vast?
My Heart has the abyss never last…

Flowers don't be so proud on your beauty
My Heart has already won the crown of cutie…

You say the Zeus the God of Gods?
My Heart has the power that charms all bards…

O my breath please go slow
My Heart is so tender to bear the flow…

~ Lieutenant Vinodkumar Ashok Pradhan

63

Arindam Roy

Arindam Roy has over four decades of experience in various newsrooms. He is the founder, Publishing Director, and Editor-in-Chief of Different Truths and KKPC, the publishing wing. He held senior positions in several media houses and has worked as a mainstream journalist. He co-authored ten chapters in six Coffee Table Books (CTBs) of national and international repute. Of these, one was published in Milan, Italy; another was a Marg publication (Mumbai), and the Times Group published two. He is the sole author of four forthcoming CTBs (Times Group). Widely anthologised, he published three anthologies as Publisher-Editor, while three other anthologies are in the pipeline. He is a co-author of the novel *Rivers Run Back*; his writing partner is a renowned American author. He lives in Prayagraj (Allahabad) and Bangalore.

Binaries of Peace

Snug on its mother's bosom
A child sleeps, peacefully,
Unaware of the missile attacks
Or bombings in war-ravaged Ukraine –
It could be Taiwan, soon.
The infant's father, a young soldier
Sleeps peacefully in his grave:
Strange binaries of Peace!
In the silence of a full moon night
The moonbeam is still in its mirror
The large placid lake, the calm eyes
Of a Rishi, in deep meditation
At another time and place
A sage-poet composes hymns
Of peace and harmony
A Shanti Path, praying for
Peace of the living and those
Departed, known and unknown,
With or without funeral rites. He
Prays for the peace of a grass blade,
Forests, mountains, and seas,
Peace for the Earth and the Great Void
Peace for mankind, gods, and demons –
Shanti – Peace to one and all!

~ **Arindam Roy**

From the Editors' Desk
INNSÆI's Voices

Dr. Tejaswini Patil

Dr. Tejaswini Patil is Head, Dept. of English in Arts and Commerce College, Kasegaon, (Sangli, M.S.), Founder Director, INNSÆI, An International Journal of Creative Literature for Peace and Humanity. Her Marathi, Hindi and English poems have been published in 50+ national and international anthologies including South Africa, Romania, USA and UK. The poetry collections- (English) - 'Talons and Nets' translated into Romanian, 'Verses of Silence' and 'A Glass of Time' and Kaainat (Hindi) and a reference book: 'Relations and Relationship' are to her credit. She's edited 'Mystical Voices', Tunisian Asian Poetry Anthology. Her poems selected for the Rio Grande Valley International Poetry Festival, Texas, and USA. Her awards are- State Level Mahila Samajratna Lifetime Achievement Award; International level 'Master of Creative Impulse Award', the International Honor of "A Great Poet and Writer Par Excellence". Her profile is included in the famous Coffee Table Book, 25 Women of Virtue; She's Vice-President of Jagadguru Tukobaray Sahitya Parishad, Dist. Satara,(M.S.); Founder Director, Adishakti Mahila Rural Non-Agricultural Cooperative Credit Society, Karad, Dist. Satara, Maharashtra;

Honorary Chief Editor, Amhi Aksharyatri, Monthly Marathi Journal; Member, Executive Committee, Shivaji University English Teachers' Association, Kolhapur; Secretary, Tejaswini Multi-purpose Social Forum, Karad(Regd. NGO); Member, Sangeet Surya Keshavrao Bhosale Kala Akademi, Kolhapur.

They wanted her to be
 A FEMALE,
A PREY,
An OBJECT
To be used and thrown away.

Can a BULLET do that..?

~ Dr. Tejaswini Patil

75

Orbindu Ganga

Orbindu Ganga is the co-founder and editorial research director of INNSÆI Journal. He is a consultant, publisher, author, editor, poet, content writer, painter, researcher, and observer. He is a certified life coach, spiritual mentor, and creator of Subconscious Observation Belief System (SOBS), mindset coach, holistic coach, personal coach, and English Communication Trainer.

The Eleventh Hour

The blank whispered
The silence, waiting
For the ink to be kissed,
To get the colours
Ebb incessantly, garden
Of rainbow smiled to
Charm the eternity
With delight, the Sanctum
Santorum greeted the naive
To belong to the league
Favoured by the least.

Words and colours
Get misted in hue,
With a whiff of dust
Sprawling across
The desert, the waves
Are waiting for the tides
To bind the glee and grieve,
They bind in unison at the eleventh hour to travel in cumulus,
Words penned a missive
Colours decorated the canvas.

~ Orbindu Ganga

Dr Kalpana Girish Gangatirkar

Dr Kalpana Girish Gangatirkar works as an Associate Professor in Mahavir Mahavidyalaya Kolhapur, Maharashtra from 1992. Her areas of interest are Indian English Literature, New Literatures, Translation Studies, Feminist Literature, etc. She writes poetry in both English and Marathi. She is a short story writer and there is a collection of short stories entitled *Reflection* to her credit. She has participated in various International and national seminars and conferences and presented papers. Her more than 30 papers are published in International and national journals. She has worked as coordinator of international conferences and symposium and edited journals.

Pursuit of Peace

I struggled and strived hard,
became a part of rat-race,
fulfilled each of my desire
and secured every pleasure.
I achieved name and fame
and won this never ending game.
But alas! My agitating soul
was still unrest and moil.

Then to seek the peace of heart
I embraced my darlings and dears
But oh! They exchanged fears,
aches, woes and distress pierce.
I turned away from them
being more and more dismayed!

In the search of serenity
I chased the path of spirituality,
listened sermons, visited temples
several times at several places,
spotted the crowds empty
priests hungry for bounty.
In the bubbling mantras' sound
the harmony and peace how can I found?

I invoked the Almighty
and urged to grant me peace.
He showed gloom and misery
the poor, wretched and needy,
I served and wiped their tears

Aditi Barve

Aditi Barve is the Head of the Department of English at Srinivassa Sinai Dempo Colllege of Commerce and Economics Goa. She writes in English, Marathi, Hindi and Konkani. She conducts workshops titled- 'Happy Exams' ; 'Importance of English Language and how to be fluent in English'. Govt. of Maharshtra conferred the prestigious Brihanmaharashtra Award for her translation.

Buddha! We Need You Again

Buddha, we need you again.
Morality, compassion is in draught
we need some metta and
the panchasheel that you taught.

May we follow
the precept of not killing,
abstinence from intoxicants
should be our heart's willing.

To the significant other,
faithful may we be;
and speak only the truth,
may falsehood just flee.

May we not pick up
what does not belong to us,
abstinence from stealing
we do achieve thus.

If only we understand
the cause and effect theory
then we shall stop
being restless and weary.

When one is agitated and worried
everyone around is in woe.
Humanity attains peace
when every individual does so

Beyond this, let there be
compassion in our minds
towards our own species
and with all the other kinds

May we understand anichcha…
the impermanence of everything.
Our world is called bhavsagar
because it is always becoming

May we fight against
the habit of aversion and craving.
May we overflow with gratitude
and pure love that is lifesaving.

Life Starts at Forty

Once I felt that
I had not achieved anything
I started disliking myself
while in the whirlpool of overthinking.
Aditi, life starts at forty.
A friend once told
I felt that the friend was
little harsh and cold...
Nevertheless, I realised that
life was like a swain
It started again like
yearly monsoon rain

Life actually starts
whenever you want it to start
so my dear sisters
it is time to be alert and smart.
If you are forty five
come out of your bee hive
enjoy every moment
It is your life, you drive.
If you are sixty,
celebrate that you are living
enjoy every moment now
that you wasted once – overthinking.
Life starts at any age
just allow it to bloom
Listen to your heart
do away with the gloom
Sisters you are the light
of the rising sun
So you all deserve
loads of peace and fun
Do not wait for
some special day

Life starts here and now
Start it now, in your way.

~ Aditi Barve

87

Sweta Kumari

Sweta Kumari (Gold Medalist, M.A. & NET in English) is a bilingual national and international award-winning poet, short story writer, avid reader, an editor and an anthology compiler. Currently, she is pursuing her PhD research project entitled "Dialectics of Feminism in Select Hindi Films and Film Adaptations of Indian English Novels (1960-2010)". Her areas of interest are Contemporary issues like Women Empowerment, Patriarchy, Post-Colonial Studies, Feminism and Film Studies. Besides, she has presented several scholarly papers in national and international seminars/conferences and participated actively in workshops. Moreover, her research papers got published in several reputed national and international Journals, seminar proceedings and in edited books. She is an editorial Board member of Global Literati Insight Research Journal and *Innsaei: An International Journal of Creative Literature, Art Translation and Research for Peace and Humanity* as well as the regional Director of Bihar of Suryodaya Literary Foundation. Writings brought some more accolades and awards as inspiration to her, and she has been awarded several national and international awards including Father Day Presentation 2019 Best Budding Poet of The

Year" and a certificate for "Outstanding Performance Poetry Recitation Award" by the Literati Council, India in an International Conference on Widow's Problem and Their Solutions. She has also been awarded with several awards like "Rashtriya Ratna Award-2019", "Rajastariye Prabodhan Thakre Samajsudharak Purushkar-2019", "Uttar Pradesh Ratna Shaman-2019", "Literoma Laureate in Best Aspiring Author Award-2019", "Film & Literature 1st Corporate Ceremony- International Indian Award in Literature-2020", "Nobel Laureate Kabi Rabindranath Tagore Award-2020", and "Women of the Year-2020" etc. Moreover, she edited and published several book anthologies titled *A Date with Poetry* (2019), *Voices from the Society-Vol-1* and *Vol-2, Incentive, Lockdown-14, Akiriti: Badalte Pahlu, Snaps of Scintillating Souls* and *Polyphony of Women's Odyssey, Efflorescence: A Florilegium of Humanity, Nature and Peace, Symphony of Words: A Poetic Collection* and *Literature and Arts for Peace and Humanity Research Papers Presented in the INNSÆI LIT Fest, Goa 2022* . You can connect with her on Instagram at @sweta5259, Facebook- Sweta Kumai and Twitter- Sweta Kumari

Mellifluous Musings: A Healing to Scars

She- a free soul walks in solid spheres,
The universe, the creator and the perpetuators,
Of ages, generations to come.
Though subjugated, enslaved, and oppressed on and on,
However, battling the patriarchal battlefield,
From the ashes of her life; still she rises like a phoenix,
No matter the countless times, she breaks down,
After every defeat, there's for Her A New Dawn.

A sunrise at Her dusky time,
To bestow the space to thrive,
No darkness in her to prevail,
No more an age to enslave,
No wonder, if the stories remain unsaid,
A time to unveil all ingrained notions ahead.
No where the shadow of the past to dwell,
As all the scars obliterated as dead shells,
The age of fetters just came dead,
The imprisoned thoughts for Her slowly fade.

A renaissance in woman's life,
Adoring wings with freedom to fly,
Cherishing their divine empyrean dream,
Where to be heard no silent screams.
Though, myriad voices through individual mellifluous
musings,
To validate the realm for an equal footing,
Where to breathe free-spirited and to lead,
The undefined world of self-esteem.

A new birth of her uncaged dreams,
Being sung the song of Free Rein,
A conqueror of the realm of diabolic affairs,
Creating the solemn saga of the present flair.
Beholding the world in its own downstream,
Demasking the countless countenance,
Of their struggles in the tenacious tales,
To recount the voyage of all shackled souls,
Divulging the more of the sides in whole.

~ Sweta Kumari